ONCE UPON A DREAM

Beyond Imagination

Edited By Wendy Laws

First published in Great Britain in 2019 by:

Young Writers
Remus House
Coltsfoot Drive
Peterborough
PE2 9BF
Telephone: 01733 890066
Website: www.youngwriters.co.uk

FOREWORD

Welcome Reader, to a world of dreams.

For Young Writers' latest competition, we asked our writers to dig deep into their imagination and create a poem that paints a picture of what they dream of, whether it's a make-believe world full of wonder or their aspirations for the future.

The result is this collection of fantastic poetic verse that covers a whole host of different topics. Let your mind fly away with the fairies to explore the sweet joy of candy lands, join in with a game of fantasy football, or you may even catch a glimpse of a unicorn or another mythical creature. Beware though, because even dreamland has dark corners, so you may turn a page and walk into a nightmare!

Whereas the majority of our writers chose to stick to a free verse style, others gave themselves the challenge of other techniques such us acrostics and rhyming couplets. We also gave the writers the option to compose their ideas in u story, so watch out for those narrative pieces too!

Each piece in this collection shows the writers' dedication and imagination – we truly believe that seeing their work in print gives them a well-deserved boost of pride, and inspires them to keep writing, so we hope to see more of their work in the future!

CONTENTS

Greenleas Primary School, Wallasey

Miah Simpson (10)	56
Oliver Dodd-Hughes (10)	58
Calum Dixie Jones (10)	59
Sophie Louise Smith (10)	60
Leo Le Lievre (10)	61
Kelly Nelson (10)	62

Hafren Junior School, Newtown

Oliver Powell (11)	63
Emma Kuegler (11)	64
Kolvet Gwilt (11)	65
Scarlet Ela (11)	66

Hampton Dene Primary School, Hampton Dene

Ty Bromley (10)	67
Jarvis Apperley (9)	68
Jesse Slancauskas (9)	69
Max Thomas (9)	70

Holy Cross Catholic Primary School, Liverpool

Suba Keerthika Ramachandran (9)	71
Fatema Abdulbaset Qahtan (9)	72
Aleena Thanawala (10)	73
Miley-May Broadhurst (9)	74

Holy Spirit Catholic Primary School, Parr

Lucy-Jo Anders (10)	75
Bella Leah Ody (9)	76

Southdown Primary School, Buckley

Amélie Roberts (10)	78
Lilia Molica-Franco (10)	80

Mia Broughton	82
Milly-May Griffiths	84
Lilyann Braithwaite (10)	85
Nia Evans	86
Tayla Tattersall	87
Evie Cosgrove	88

St Andrew's CE (VC) Primary School, Bulmer

Amy Elizabeth Russell (8)	89
Emmy Lorraine (8)	90
Alfie Caleb Jones (10)	91
Orla Beau Sibley (8)	92
Rubi Jean Chappell (8)	93
Charlie Banks (10)	94
Tommy Frederick Chappell (10)	95
Connor Bickmore (11)	96
Justin Brown (10)	97
Thomas James Garden (8)	98
Logan Pressling (10)	99
George Griffiths (9)	100

St Joseph The Worker Catholic Primary School, Southdene

Faye Elizabeth Joyce Burke (11)	101

St Patrick's CE Primary School, Endmoor

Daniel James Gardner (10)	103
Holly Ellis (9)	104
Poppy Easterlow (10)	105
Erin Munford (9)	106
Ben Morris (9)	107
Abby Mason (10)	108
Samantha Taylor (8)	109
Kieran Collier (9)	110

Tattingstone Primary School, Tattingstone

Chloe Tuan Darcy-Langley (10)	111
Olive Potter-Cobbold (11)	112
Faith Davy (9)	113
Jack Harry Hemsley Cooper (8)	114
Francesca Goodwin (11)	115
Samuel Cocksedge (10)	116
Daisy Kemp (9)	117
James Moore (10)	118
Aggie Cook (9)	119
Charles Peter Hemsley Cooper (10)	120

Templeton CP School, Templeton

Poppy Louise Marion Kirkwood (10)	121

Tonysguboriau Primary School, Talbot Green

Harry Howell (9)	122

Trowell CE Primary School, Trowell

Elias Wright (10)	123
Aidan Smart (10)	124
Poppy Gow (10)	126
Rosanna Race (10)	128
Ava Byrne (9)	130
Millie Concannon (10)	132
Hannah Martin (10)	134
Theo James Morgan (10)	135
Leila Burt (10)	136
Ben Small (10)	138
Tia-Madison Ingham (10)	139
Logan Jones (10)	140
Charlie Partridge (10)	142
Rosie Turnbull (10)	143
Clarice Edmonds (10)	144
Bella Marie Turner (10)	145
Poppy Potts-Padgett (9)	146

Mohammad Ali Saddique (10)	147
Freya Noakes (9)	148

Victoria Junior School, Workington

Ruby Grace Cowan (8)	149
Aimee Marie Benson (7)	150
Summer Carr (7)	151
Alisha Hussain (8)	152
Blake Dakin (8)	153
Julia Kuder (8)	154
CJ Moore	155
Alaiya Richardson (8)	156
Lacey-Leigh Harding (7)	157
Archie Smitham (7)	158
Song Song Chen (8)	159
Kyron Knowles (8)	160

West Grantham Academy St John's, Grantham

Lily Bavister (8)	161
Roksana Osowska (8)	162

Wyndham Primary Academy, Alvaston

Annabel Syme (8)	163
Sophia Sylvia (7)	164
Alvin Nkwelle (8)	165
Toby Elijah Walsh (7)	166
Gabrielle Orunmuyi (8)	167
Julia Cybulska (8)	168
Beth Rule (8)	169
Laura Viktorija Klaveniece (7)	170
Kelsey Biddle (8)	171
Lily-May Wosik (8)	172
Lily Harrison (8)	173
Emily Neimane (8)	174
Michael Turner (8)	175
Dylan Adkins (8)	176
Harry Woolley (8)	177
John Holmes (8)	178

Cole Ingman (8)	179
Rakeisha Vuyelwa Mutandi (8), Edgar & Nenidawh	180
Jonatan Domzala (8)	181
Marlie James Doniel Shields (8)	182
Alfie Welch (7)	183
Isabelle Saxby (8)	184
Olly Benjamin (8)	185
Keegan Morris (8)	186

Ysgol Parcyrhun, Ammanford

Arrin Riccards (9)	187
Olivia Tozer (11)	188
Harriet Tozer (8)	189
Olivia Anne Griffiths (8)	190

THE POEMS

Dreams

D rifting into a silent slumber
R udely disturbed by rumbles of thunder
E erie shadows fill the room
A cackling witch flies past on a broom
M onsters chase me, I can't help but scream
S uddenly I wake up, it was just a dream.

Tamzin Evans (10)
Aberdare Park Primary School, Trecynon

The Worst Dream

T here was a zombie staring right in my little eyes,

H ere was me and him, glaring at each other outside with our pies,

E veryone was screaming, "Argh! Where's my baby?" I was thinking, *where's the gravy.*

W e started to chase each other

O ver and again, he got close to catching me,

R esting my legs inside of an abandoned water park,

S ilently, I found an old man lying down, I jumped,

T he zombie grabbed the old man and ate him in a flash. I was the only person alive.

D are I fight the zombies?

"R un," a voice said, "run."

E ven the old man turned into a zombie.

A t the break of dawn, they grabbed me.

M y room was silent as I looked around.

Lucy McGill (10)
Cefn Fforest Primary School, Cefn Fforest

Fire Vs Ice

Birds and police are all I can see,
Fire is shooting out of me,
Suddenly, I notice I have shields and blades,
I try to run away but my dreams make me stay.

I smash the ground and destroy everyone,
The police crouch down and pull out their guns,
Mr Freeze tries to blow
But in the process, he ruins the show.

I shoot fire left and right,
All Mr Freeze is left with is a fright,
He tries to conquer my burning hands,
But instead, he melts down to sand.

Swiftly, I wake up in my bed
All I knew was in my head,
In my dream, I felt like steel,
But then again, none of it was real.

Edward Deane-Calnan (11)
Cefn Fforest Primary School, Cefn Fforest

The Dream I Went To Space

Last night, I had a dream
There was something beaming

I was on the floor
I looked up and there was a door

I got up and looked around
There was no ground

I was in space
It was a peaceful place

I drifted off
Until we stopped

I saw the galaxy
I called my friend, Maxie

We saw an asteroid shooting
Like a footballer booting

Oh, look! There is a cheese river
Can I get a slither?

This is an epic rocket
Quick, lock it!

Oh no! It was getting out of control
Nervous excitement in my soul!

I woke up in a rush
A slush would be lush

I ran downstairs
Like no one cared

I had a slush
And it was lush!

Violet Grace Cassley-Doak (10)
Cefn Fforest Primary School, Cefn Fforest

Best Birthday Dream

B est birthday ever,
I had a kitten for my birthday,
R osie was her name,
T he food was delicious like a candy cane.
H ow could I possibly ask for more?
D ays I've been planning this.
A fter the DJ came we were partying like mad.
"Y ay," everyone screamed, it was the best birthday.

D ays I dreamed about having this party.
R ose petals flew through the air.
E veryone was screaming, "Hip hip hooray."
A big cheer came when I blew out my candles.
M y birthday party was the best.

Holly Agland (11)
Cefn Fforest Primary School, Cefn Fforest

Wind Flower, The Powerful Unicorn

Come back, Miss Unicorn,
I can see you in the soft and silky clouds,
Your light pink hair softly swaying in the air
And your yellow and pink ombre tail,
I can see you miles away.

Your golden horn sparkles and is as swirly as a snake,
You make me forget about my nightmares,
Let me fly away on your smooth, white back,
Flying me up to the light blue sky.

I suddenly feel this feeling inside me,
Then I hear the jingling bells.
"Is that Santa?" I say.
I feel quite frightened.

But then I think, *this must be a dream.*

Rihanna John (10)
Cefn Fforest Primary School, Cefn Fforest

Football

F erociously, I run down the left-wing dangerously

O n top of the luscious, green grass.

O ver the top of the defenders, a risky slide tackle, I jump.

"T op corner now!" The crowd cheer at my screamer of a goal.

B ehind me, my teammates jump up and down.

A ll of the crowd erupt whilst the goalkeeper screams in frustration.

L ights as bright as the sun dazzle their manager.

L aughter spreads like a Mexican wave at my awesome celebration.

Logan Sadler (11)
Cefn Fforest Primary School, Cefn Fforest

The Fierce Dragon

Once upon a dream
I couldn't believe what I had seen,
A fierce dragon who trapped Alexander,
In order to beat him, I must be faster.

In a blink of an eye, I picked up my sword,
Impoverished and defenceless he was, he was bored,
So I sped things up,
Like I was a beaming pup.

Alexander found the rusty key
And randomly threw it at me,
In a dash, I slew the creature,
In my room, his skull would be a triumphant feature.

William Rhys Landrygan (10)
Cefn Fforest Primary School, Cefn Fforest

Dreaming Of Juventus!

J uvenile players train day in, day out to be the best in the league,

U nder lots of pressure.

V alencia trying their hardest to defeat our solid defence.

E ven any English teams are no match for us!

N o team can defeat us!

T housands of fans cheering us on.

U nbelievable! Ronaldo absolutely smashes the ball into the back of the net!

S creams are all you can hear as Juventus win yet another match!

Morgan Marozzelli (11)
Cefn Fforest Primary School, Cefn Fforest

Killer Clowns

Once upon a night
Walking through the forest,
Sometimes gave me a fright,
Screaming was coming from the darkness.

I followed the sound
And to my surprise,
A young 17-year-old girl,
Tied to the trees and the ground.

"Help! Help! Help!" she cried.
I didn't know what to do.
I pulled at the chains and tried,
There was nothing I could do.

Joshua Leigh Harris (11)
Cefn Fforest Primary School, Cefn Fforest

Jumping

J umps all around, it was our time to compete

"**U** p!" I encouraged Lady to go.

M y heart pounds. I hope we have a clear round.

P ractise, practise, practise, is all we have done.

I finished the round, it was clean.

N othing has stopped us, I pray that we have won.

G old is ours, I can't believe we did it.

Lacey Louise Matthews (11)
Cefn Fforest Primary School, Cefn Fforest

The Canvas

As I grip onto the soft, fluffy brushes,
Reds, oranges, blues and pinks fill my canvas.
Thinking of a beautiful design
I scribble away at my canvas.
Surprisingly my creation
Turns into colourful flowers.
As I let my imagination run wild
The flowers soon become alive.
Amazed and shocked, I peacefully stare,
I am proud.

Madison Mathews (11)
Cefn Fforest Primary School, Cefn Fforest

Clowns

C oming face to face with my biggest fear,
L ying on my bed, hoping my parents are near.
O h no, I hope they don't come,
W hy can't you get rid of them with the hit of a drum?
N o, no, no, they have come. "Help!"
S ometimes I wish they would leave on their own.

Libby May (11)
Cefn Fforest Primary School, Cefn Fforest

14

Football

Running around the pitch,
Getting my blood pumping.

People around me
Watching me play.

Liverpool in front,
I'm surrounded by blue.

But my problem is
What should I do?

Liverpool want to sign me,
I need to decide.

I'm torn between the two.

Kai Brooklyn Thomas (11)
Cefn Fforest Primary School, Cefn Fforest

Fortnite

F alling off the bus
O nto the island
R egretting everything
T o the place known as Neo Tilted
N ight coming
I got four kills
T ilted is in a storm
E nd of the game, I win.

Jay David Parfitt (11)
Cefn Fforest Primary School, Cefn Fforest

Thanos

T he mad Titan

H as conquered the world

A nd destroyed Wakanda

N o one can stop him

O nly the great Captain Marvel

S uddenly Captain Marvel uses her mega-blast and kills Thanos!

Lewis John Haddock (11)

Cefn Fforest Primary School, Cefn Fforest

The Mystery Of The Actor

"Three, two, one, and action!" *Boom!* The lights flashed. The people who were not meant to be on set dashed. The set was in Godric's Hollow.

Five hours later, the director called, "Done, for now, go back home, have a rest and then your acting skills will be the best."

I arrived at home. My house was an expensive, marble white house in Hollywood with fifteen pools and nine hot tubs.

Ding-dong!

Who could that be at my door? I opened my door and what a surprise. It was Daniel Radcliffe. This wouldn't give me a bore. We sat on the couch to talk about my new pouch. My phone gave a call.

"It's Emma," I exclaimed. "You want me to come to the set? Okay."

So off I set in my golden Lamborghini that was as shiny as a diamond.

When I arrived at the set, Bonnie Wright said, "Read this letter!"

The letter danced around in my hand and started to talk. It shouted, "Help, I'm in Hogsmeade, I have been kidnapped by Tom Felton. Please help. Thank you, Daniel."

Then the letter ripped itself up.

"Oh no, poor Daniel, let's go and get him!"

Poof!

We teleported to Hogsmeade. We started looking on the ground and saw a picture.

"Is it a clue?" Emma said curiously.

"Yes, oh boy, it's the three broomsticks' logo, let's go there right now, we have got to save Daniel."

Boom!

We teleported again and found ourselves face to face with Daniel.

Boom!

We teleported again and found ourselves face to face with Tom Felton.

"Let him go, you foulsome, evil little cockroach!" screamed Emma.

"Calm down, Emma," said Felton with an evil grin. "He is here, no need to worry, but first answer this riddle. I was used often in the olden days but now I am in an electronic device. What am I?"

I laughed. "Oh Tom, you have said this riddle loads of times, it's Google Maps."

"Oh fine, here he is."

Tom looked very disappointed.

"Quick, grab him." We grabbed Daniel and we teleported back to the set.

Poof!

We were home, everyone sighed in relief but we would never know who the fake actor was!

Gracie Green (9)
Forest Glade Primary School, Sutton-In-Ashfield

The Frightening Night

This morning, I woke up in my bed,
I had a dream, I was filled with dread.
I got up out of bed,
I had a strange feeling about my mum
So I went downstairs to get my morning snack.
Down the stairs I went, I saw my mum in her mac,
Sat on the stairs,
I sat next to her, I looked at her face,
I couldn't believe my eyes,
She was covered in blood.
I shouted to my dad, but he was dead.
I grabbed Mum's phone and called the police,
As soon as the police came
I went to the station.
I was sat there in the room where they question you.
He put on his recorder thing.
Boop, it went on for a while
And when it stopped, he talked.
"Did you see or hear anything?" the inspector asked me.
"No, I was asleep," I said.
"Okay, did you see anyone?" he asked.
"No!" I screamed. "I just said I was asleep."

Tehya (8)
Forest Glade Primary School, Sutton-In-Ashfield

Champions League Final

In the Santiago Bernabéu, the Champions League final
Where Man City take on Liverpool.
The game has started and its an early chance for Sterling
But Alisson tips it round the post.
Now it's a corner, David Silva takes
And Laporte headers it into the net.
Firmino shoots, Ederson saves,
It goes out to Mo Salah
And he scores to make it 1-1.
Agüero chips it over the keeper's head and makes it 2-1.

Penalty to make it 2-2.
Origi shoots and scores.
50th minute, Bernardo Silva shoots but gets fouled,
Sané takes the free kick, he shoots,
Scores from thirty-five yards, it goes into the top corner.
Sané gets his 100th goal of Man City
And puts them 3-2 up.

It's Mo Salah in the 73rd minute
And he scores to make it 3-3.
Agüero is in on goal, he shoots and scores

And makes it 4-3 and gets a hat-trick.
Now it's Sané, he scores and makes it 5-3
And the whistle goes and Man City win the Champions
League.

George Peter Cockerill (8)

Forest Glade Primary School, Sutton-In-Ashfield

The Jellybean Spider

J ellybeans are as revolting as poop to me,
E ven though spiders are smaller than me, I am as frightened as can be.
L ovely as they are, the jellybean spider is kinder than all,
L oving and caring as much as she can,
Y et my friends are scared of her, we are the best of friends,
B ut now every ebony-black night, my friends and I visit her in Candy Land,
E very night she gives us a fright but we still love her either way,
A ll her love and kindness is stronger than all,
N ight and day, colourful and bright.

S pontaneous little spider shining in the night,
P etrifying creature, but very sweet,
I 'll love her for evermore,
D eep down in my heart, I will never forget,
E very night, I see her,
R uling the Jellybean Kingdom together.

Ella-May Cresswell-Hibbert (9)
Forest Glade Primary School, Sutton-In-Ashfield

Sweet Land Saved

S weet Land needs to be saved!

W ill we defeat the dreaded witch

E ven though we have seven people willing to fight?

E ven though they are not strong enough

T o cast a blinding spell.

L east of all is the spell called

A crobats, Anna is able to do that spell.

N ow, I think they need to come to the gingerbread house.

D oor of toffee, candyfloss carpet, lollipop chimney, liquorice roof.

I s this working?

S o Else and Hermione are standing still just as I thought.

S o turn around Olaf, Kristoff, Sven, Ana and Nicola.

A s always, it works, they have defeated the dreaded witch.

V ictoria, the sweet witch will be happy.

E ven though you will win,

D read never started! You were tested!

Nicola Bird (9)
Forest Glade Primary School, Sutton-In-Ashfield

It's Dance

Today, I go to dance,
I'm going to do the hardest dance in the world.
Oh no, I can't do the hardest dance in the world
Because I've got a competition and I haven't practised.
Wait, I still remember how to do one dance.
I better start practising.
I now need to go and get on my dance costume.
I know what song I'm dancing to, it's... oh, I forgot.
I hope my friends know what I'm dancing to.
I wish this dance had a part where you could dance
with a friend instead of dancing on your own.
In this competition, whoever wins gets a free passport
to Paris.
I really hope I win this competition.
Now I'm going to go onto the sparkly stage.
Oh yes, my best friend in the whole world won,
I'm so, so happy for her.
She said she can take me with her to Paris.

Kaicie Woolley
Forest Glade Primary School, Sutton-In-Ashfield

Mythical Jungle

Whoosh! Me and my friends are lost in the jungle!
Now we are in a really big jumble!
I can't believe my eyes!
I'm covered in sparkly flies!

Oh! What else is there?
Look! There are four unicorns playing, so fair!
There is a bunny who wears a stripy tie!
There is a Pegasus flying so high!

What is that?
Is that a tall top hat?
There is a secret door!
With a sparkly, shiny, yellow floor!

The animals open a hatch!
They say, "Get ready to catch!"
Then I see what they mean!
I get ready to clench!
The little unicorn that flew into my hand!
There is a big, black, green, dark land!
With a big, green, gooey, monstrous monster!

Lexi-Tai Drury (9)
Forest Glade Primary School, Sutton-In-Ashfield

The Football Match

The team entered the pitch, the whistle blew,
18th minute, the fans shouted, "Woo!"
One of the player's shirts was ripped,
All the shoes were badly clipped,
Penalty given, very slow, very quiet
Your mum shouts, "Wow!"

30th minute, they were ready to score,
But then they realised they were losing by four.
Kyle Walker funnily got mugged,
I think his wife wanted a pug.
50th minute, the ball had popped,
One of the players looked like a mop.
75th minute, a sub went on,
Now they finally scored one.
All the players were all exhausted,
Now they needed a cup and saucer.
Liverpool won 4-1!

Harry James (9)
Forest Glade Primary School, Sutton-In-Ashfield

Magical Creators

The people who make the sun shine,
The people who paint the colours on my rainbow,
The people who salt the seas,
The people who give the moon its glow.

The people who splatter colours,
On the sunset and sunrise,
The people who puff up the shape-shifting clouds,
The people who blue the skies.

The people who make the icicles clear,
The people who scatter shimmering stars,
The people who whiten the sleeping snow
And spread magic on this wonderful world of ours.

The people who bloom the flowers,
The people we never see,
They're as magical as anything,
I wonder what their next spell will be.

Hannah Paterson (9)
Forest Glade Primary School, Sutton-In-Ashfield

I Adopted...

On Monday, I adopted a dog,
The dog ran, jumped and bounced.
On Tuesday, I adopted a bunny,
The bunny jumped my obstacle course.
On Wednesday, I adopted a cat,
It scratched my walls and woke me up.

On Thursday, I adopted a mouse,
It went *squeak, squeak*
And made so much noise I could barely even breathe.
On Friday, I adopted a horse,
It went *neigh, neigh* and started to eat my hay.

On Saturday, I adopted a guinea pig,
It ate my apples and ate my lettuce that I was going to
have for my tea.
On Sunday, I adopted my dog's brother!
He was the perfect pet for me!

Miley Ann Bingham (8)
Forest Glade Primary School, Sutton-In-Ashfield

Police Vs Clowns

P olice will fight to help the people.

O h, easy, thieves don't last long.

L ong day at work but I won't give up.

I ndependent but only sometimes, today I'm not.

C ool car, cool job.

E legant police officers are the best drivers.

V ans are everywhere.

S cary night tonight.

C reepy clowns everywhere.

L ying is their favourite thing.

O n the roof of a building.

W hy are they doing this?

N ow I'm scared,

S o hard to defeat them.

Jamie Paul Perrin (9)
Forest Glade Primary School, Sutton-In-Ashfield

The Adventure Of Unicorns

Neigh! The unicorns went into the forest,
But then they found Morris.
He was covered in goo
And was stinky too.

"Don't hurt him, he's new,
Give him a ride even though he smells like the loo."
Gracie arrived dressed like Luna's daughter from Harry Potter
And was extraordinary at making unicorn's trotters.

Hannah arrived in a white, silky, glittery dress that was flowing behind her on a unicorn,
Stroking the unicorn's horn,
They bathed the unicorn's mane
And then they played an awesome game.

Faye Kirk (9)
Forest Glade Primary School, Sutton-In-Ashfield

The Fairies

F lying in the sky like a beautiful flower

A nne the fairy running slow, what a nice sight to see

I n Fairy Land, the fairies fly to their cottage

R unning about to the beach

I n Fairy Land, the fairies fly in the dark sky

E nergetic, the fairies are flying to New Zealand

S ilently, the fairies wake up, ready to start the day.

Lacey Wright (9)

Forest Glade Primary School, Sutton-In-Ashfield

The Goalkeeper

G oalkeepers save goals
O ff the line saves
A bove the bar
L ots of clean sheets
K nowing that you just saved a penalty kick
E nd of the game
E nd of the league that you just won
P eople invade the pitch
E nd of the party
R un home, it will do you good.

Charlie Dawes (9)
Forest Glade Primary School, Sutton-In-Ashfield

In The Land Of Make-Believe

Far away
We play,
Harry Potter is our game,
Dragons tame,
Harry came.

Spells and wands,
Wave our hands,
All together make a spell.

Hocus pocus,
Potions and emotions,
In my Land of Make-Believe.

Cauldrons, potions,
Mix them up,
Spellbooks,
We must look.

Jayden Bryce (9)
Forest Glade Primary School, Sutton-In-Ashfield

I Can't Find A Slave

R oyalty, royalty, I love royalty

O n Tuesday, I go to my castle

Y ou don't know how hard it is to find a slave

A ll day long, I can't find a slave

L alalala, I can't find a slave

T uesday, I go to my castle

Y ou don't know how hard it is to find a slave.

Isabel Niamh Campbell (8)
Forest Glade Primary School, Sutton-In-Ashfield

There Once Was A Man With A Frown

There once was a man with a frown
Who looked like a scary clown.
He liked to sell balloons,
He sold them 'til noon.

There once was a man with a frown
Who looked like a scary clown.
He came back into town
And earned more money and lost his frown.

Max Flint (9)
Forest Glade Primary School, Sutton-In-Ashfield

Joker

J okes around every day like a tomato in a shop
O h, I don't know what to say
K illing Batman is my thing
E asy killing, not afraid
R eclaiming glory, like a man.

Owen Woodland (8)
Forest Glade Primary School, Sutton-In-Ashfield

Unicorns

Once upon a dream
I bumped into a beautiful, elegant unicorn,
It was as white as snow.

I was shocked.
I expected it to be timid and quiet
But it was as loud as an elephant's scream.

I could see its magnificent rainbow mane
And its shimmering golden horn.
It was like a shining, shimmering star.
The grass tickled my feet, I was so surprised.

I could smell all the fabulous flowers around
As they smelt like very strong and powerful perfumes.

I picked up a little, pink flower from the ground.
I could taste a little bit of it in my mouth, it tickled.
My whole entire mouth went all weird and soft.

I could feel the soft, fluffy fur of the unicorn.
I was so satisfied and amazed.
I was so happy and excited that all at once, I woke up
And my dream ended.

Iarina Stefania Miron (9)
Goodly Dale Primary School, Windermere

Fairy Land

Once upon a dream
I touched a soft door
And when I opened it, it yawned.
Once upon a dream
I tasted fairy food
And it was as soft as marshmallows.
Once upon a dream
I breathed in the hot air
And it burnt my throat.
Once upon a dream
I gazed up to the stars
And they were incredibly bright.
Once upon a dream
I dreamt about my adventure to Fairy Land
And finally meeting the Fairy Queen.

Katie Milligan (8)
Goodly Dale Primary School, Windermere

Dancing Galaxy

Once upon a dream
I awoke in an enormous galaxy
Where the colours splashed and crashed inside my
eyes.
I was surprised and shocked.

I heard the sun explode like a gunshot through glass.
I saw stars glittering like diamonds in the night.

The galaxy air smelt of vanilla ice cream.
I could touch the thick air with my fingertips.
It felt like I was dipping my hand into sand.

Charlie Taylor (9)
Goodly Dale Primary School, Windermere

The Crowded Beach

I awoke on a burning beach as hot as fire.
The seagulls squawked as loud as foghorns.
It was as though they were perched on my shoulders.

The roaring waves crashed against the rocks,
They seemed furious.

The smell of mussels, scattered on the rocks
Was so strong I could almost taste them.

My mouth tasted salty and dry.
I awoke in bed, as parched as the desert.

Arthur Kirby (9)
Goodly Dale Primary School, Windermere

The Dream Of All Dreams

I was in beautiful Bird Land.
At the king's palace, the king was an eagle.
As a gift, I was given a glistening owl feather.
It glowed softly with a golden light
Whilst a blue tit perched upon my shoulder.
I sat by the magical river listening to the birds singing
all around me.
Sadly, my journey was just a dream
But I still had the glistening feather dancing in my
hand.

Emily Bruce (8)
Goodly Dale Primary School, Windermere

The Waterfall

Once upon a dream
I travelled in a caravan to a magic waterfall.
I could hear the waterfall splashing down to the pool of
calm water.
I could see the mermaids waving their sparkling tails.
I could smell the sweet scent of soft, red rosemary.
I could taste the horrible stench of a troll, as stinky as a
sock.
A prickly thorn bush grabbed me and I shouted,
"Ouch!"

Phea Niamh Tyson (8)
Goodly Dale Primary School, Windermere

Noisy Zootropolis

I arrived by a magical portal at noisy Zootropolis.
All the animals gazed into my eyes.
I heard a huge bang!
An incredibly loud elephant trumpeted like a trombone.
I saw a wise owl who hooted so loud, the world shook.
I ate a chicken that was hot, sweet and tasty.
An enormous bear hugged me close.
It was just like my mum did yesterday!

Honzik Štecher (9)
Goodly Dale Primary School, Windermere

The Amazing Football Match!

I dreamt I was at the amazing Leicester City stadium!
I could hear the crowd cheering
And chanting in my ear.
The ball banged into the back of the net.
The tall players raced about on the huge pitch.
I smelt the fresh-cut grass wafting my way.
The warm hot dog melted in my mouth.
The soft seats cushioned me.
"Goal!"

Lily Rose Backhouse (8)
Goodly Dale Primary School, Windermere

My Space Adventure

Once upon a dream,
I travelled up to sparkling space
And floated all around,
It was awesome!

I heard rockets whooshing by
And space speaking to me.

Gooey green aliens argued and shouted.
The space air smelt of black liquorice.

I touched the ring around Jupiter
And believe it was all real.

Amelia Gooden (7) & Ainhoa Gonzalez (9)
Goodly Dale Primary School, Windermere

Autumn's Amazing Chocolate Factory

Once upon a dream
I fell into a chocolate fountain,
As hot as the sun.
Once upon a dream
I tasted the chocolate
And it tingled on my tongue.
Once upon a dream
I swam in the chocolate
And breathed in its silky smell.
Once upon a dream
I gazed at the chocolate
And admired its golden sheen.

Autumn Parkingson Chapman (7)
Goodly Dale Primary School, Windermere

Once Upon A Magical Land

Strolling through a forest, I fell through a hole.
Arriving at a chocolate castle, I became as cold as ice.
Talking raspberry ripple and dancing plates.
Where was I?
Hearing the eerie sound of ghosts,
I escaped in a candy cane rocket.
Whooshing through the air, I flew back to my bed.
Was it all a dream?

Pablo Nunez de Castro (9)
Goodly Dale Primary School, Windermere

My Journey To The Moon

I travelled to the grey, rocky moon
With craters as big as volcanoes!

I heard my feet stomping like a huge giant.

The moon spoke to me
And golden stars shone down like the sun in the sky.

The edges of each crater
Rippled like waterdrops on a pond.

Once upon a dream.

Erica Lindsay Rosa Beattie (8)
Goodly Dale Primary School, Windermere

Magical Land

I was in Dreamland,
I met a talking rainbow
And a unicorn as big as a mountain.

I saw stars twinkling like fairy lights.
Alicorns flew around me
And dolphins jumped above me.

I smelt the magical chocolate soup
That my mummy made me.

Once upon a dream.

Evie Lofthouse (7)
Goodly Dale Primary School, Windermere

The Dream Visit To Australia

Once upon a dream
I visited amazing Australia.
It was as hot as the sun.
I could see beautiful birds flying like lazy aeroplanes.
I could touch prickly pineapples as spiky as a hedgehog.
I felt silks in the market and they spoke like giants.
Once upon a dream.

Carys Abigayle Lowe (9)
Goodly Dale Primary School, Windermere

Up And Away

Once upon a dream
I flew and arrived on top of a fluffy cloud.
A rocket ascended as fast as lightning.
I observed it when riding my cloud elegantly.
I smelt the scent of the fuel-like ashes.
All around the cloud was quiet as a mouse
And as calm as a kitten.

Paige Parkingson Chapman (9)
Goodly Dale Primary School, Windermere

Beach

I dreamt I was on the hot, sunny beach.
The whooshing waves crashed onto the sand.
The trees swished in the whistling wind.
The air smelt of fresh mint.
I enjoyed the taste of a small coconut.
I felt the refreshing, cool breeze.

Libby Walker (8)
Goodly Dale Primary School, Windermere

Magical Land

I'm in Unicorn Land
And I'm so excited!

Fairy doors bang like butterfly wings.
Starry unicorns run and race.

I taste sweet strawberries on my tongue,
Once upon a dream.

Seryn Daisy Lowe (7)
Goodly Dale Primary School, Windermere

Mythical Dream

I lower my eyes to a world only I see,
A world that's waiting just for me.
I slip into a slumber and as I drift away,
A magical world appears, a beautiful place for me to play.
I look up at the tranquil, sapphire sky,
Where the beautiful sea is soaring high.
I dip my toes into the glimmering sea,
It's a dream world where only I can be.
Out of nowhere, an alicorn appears.
I feel so happy, it brings me to tears.
As I stroke her scarlet-red mane, which sparkles in the sunlight.
She stretches out her wings, ready to take flight.
I hop up onto her back and hold tightly to her mane.
It is so exciting, more exciting than being on an aeroplane.
We soar over the sea to a little island I've never seen.
There are majestic mountains and rapid rivers, it is so lush and green.
We finally arrive at our destination, a fairy village, the perfect dream vacation.
They flutter, dance and sing a pretty song.
Every magical creature, it is there where they belong.

So each night as I lie down on my bed,
I'm filled with joy as I rest my head.
For I know the magical places only my mind can take me.
Fairies, magic and worlds just for me,
I never want to wake up from this mythical dream.

Miah Simpson (10)

Greenleas Primary School, Wallasey

The Day I Changed The Future

Once I woke up, I didn't know where,
But it was bright and colourful, I swear.
I looked around but I saw no humans
But I did see robots.
I checked, *is this a dream?*
I looked again, *no!*
I started to take a walk, I found a prison,
I looked, no way were there people in there.
Men I found, they needed to escape,
So here came my marvellous plan.
I would find a hack, open the cell
And then deactivated the robots
So the people and I could escape
To my marvellous future.

I looked around, robots, I looked again, robots!
They weren't all deactivated.
I used a hack to deactivate some.
We had to run.
There it was, the portal,
And all of the people lived.
Hooray, we did it, but not all of it.

Oliver Dodd-Hughes (10)
Greenleas Primary School, Wallasey

I Am An Athlete!

Three, two, one, go...

While I wait for it to start I have a range of emotions
tumbling inside me...
Will I make it?
Who will win?
Will I be on the podium?

As we run the 400m men's Olympic final,
I look to the right and see Bolt around twenty-five
metres in front of me.
I feel like giving up but I don't...

A fter around 300 metres I felt like giving up,
T alking to myself, I tried as hard as I could.
H urt, lots of people went down one after the other.
L onely, the people at the back rolled their eyes.
E veryone sprinted to the finish.
T old by the sound of commentary that I was
   unexpectedly first
E veryone roared as I ran through the finish line. I
   won!

Calum Dixie Jones (10)
Greenleas Primary School, Wallasey

Dreaming The Unicorn

I dreamed I saw a unicorn last night,
It rippled through the forest, pearly-white,
Breathing a moonlit silence.
Its single horn stood shining like a lance,
I saw it toss its head and snort and prance
And paw the midnight air.
Its main was like a mass of silver hair.

But suddenly, it shuddered,
It sensed my gaze,
My wondering eyes
And turned to look upon me with surprise,
Seeming to read my face and looking as if to say,
"You are not from this place, what is your business here?"

My mind was far from clear,
I could not think or speak.
Above my head, I heard the branches creak
And then, from where I stood,
I watched it flicker off into the wood,
Into the velvet space between the trees.

Sophie Louise Smith (10)
Greenleas Primary School, Wallasey

Attack Of The Water Bottle

The water bottle looks deceiving,
You would think of no such thing,
But late at night,
It gave everyone a fright!

It attacked, destroying everything in its path
And made sure everyone knew its wrath!

People shrugged it off,
They thought it was pathetic,
But boy, were they wrong!

Leo Le Lievre (10)
Greenleas Primary School, Wallasey

Dogs Are Cool, Not Like School!

Dogs are cool, not like school,
Dogs give you their paw before you go to school,
Dogs walk but do not talk,
Dogs like to lick instead of kiss,
Dogs like to sit for a treat,
Dogs fetch a stick really quick,
Dogs like to bark in the park,
Dogs like to roll like a sausage roll.
I love dogs!

Kelly Nelson (10)
Greenleas Primary School, Wallasey

The Monstersaurus Footballer

I had a dream that I went to a football pitch,
I had a dream that a monster was there,
A monstersaurus footballer.
I was scared but here he comes.
"Hello, do you and your friend want to play?"
"For starters, what's your name?"
"I am not going to tell you."
"Why not, I am your friend."
"No you're not, I have only... oh, I forgot,
Oh yeah, I was going to say I have only known you for
five minutes.
Oh, fine, my name is... I forgot."
"How have you forgotten your name?"
"I don't know how I have forgotten."
"Right, let's get on with it.
Let's do me and my friend versus you."
"Oh, excuse me, I have forgotten to tell you my name.
My name is Bob the monstersaurus."
I scored. 2-0.
"Let's go, well done Bob, I have to go back."
"Oh, okay, see you next time."
"Bye Bob."

Oliver Powell (11)
Hafren Junior School, Newtown

Floating Clouds

As I lie asleep on my bed,
I see something fluffy above my head.
It's a cloud,
Floating high and floating proud,
Beckoning me to climb on.
As soon as I'm on, I'm gone!
Soon, all the houses are a little dot,
Don't stop reading, this isn't as far as I've got.
Soon, all I see is space,
I can't wipe my surprise off my face.
Venus, Mars, Mercury and more,
Is enough to make you surprised to the core.
All of a sudden, a star flies by,
I wave at a bird riding on it and she says, "Hi!"
She says Beatrix is her name,
She asks if I can play her game.
I play with her and I look at the clock.
"It is late, goodbye!" cries Beatrix as she flies to her
flock.
My adventure is ending, it's time to sleep,
So I curl up on the cloud, nobody hears a peep.
I feel my bed and open one eye,
I look at the cloud floating high in the sky.

Emma Kuegler (11)
Hafren Junior School, Newtown

Once Upon A Lost Land

Nothing has prepared me for this Strange Land,
I take a step forward, I can see a herd of deer.
The wind is blowing with force, through the sand,
Oh goodness, this is really testing my fears.

I can see a horse,
It's prancing and dancing,
Wait, it has a horn,
As I take my last glance,
"Whoo, it's a unicorn."

I can hear the wind curling
As I see the magic whirling,
I can see the unicorn twirling
Away with the dust,
With one huge gust.

As I close my eyes
While I am lying down,
Quicker than a fly
My mum is there looking like a clown.

Kolvet Gwilt (11)
Hafren Junior School, Newtown

Dancing Deserts

I got into bed,
I was as comfortable as a kitten
And I thought of dancing deserts.
I instantly fell asleep into a deep sleep.
Everything started dancing,
Suddenly, they started flying.
I felt a little scared.
There was screaming,
Then it stopped.
It was as dark as night,
I was alone.
Suddenly, I woke up in a desert
With no water and no supplies
So I walked and walked.
I found a door so I opened it.
I was at a football match.
I didn't know how to play,
So they chased me.
I woke the next morning and never forgot it.

Scarlet Ela (11)
Hafren Junior School, Newtown

My Transforming House

My house is a transforming house!
A house that can drive,
It also can fly.
It turns to boats,
In the water, it floats,
Drifting off to sea...

It turns into a robot,
It turns into a helicopter,
Windows that I can see!

Ty Bromley (10)
Hampton Dene Primary School, Hampton Dene

Star Wars ~ Another Story

Once upon a time,
In a galaxy,
Far, far away,
There was a Jedi in a spaceship that was under attack.
The Jedi was named Jarvis.
His ship crashed into his best friend, Cody.
The team with the Jedi introduced them.

Jarvis Apperley (9)
Hampton Dene Primary School, Hampton Dene

Jesse Bought A New Car

In my dream
I went to the car shop
And I bought a blue car.
When I bought the car
I drove the car.
A normal, slow car.
Then I drove home
And I cleaned my new car.

Jesse Slancauskas (9)
Hampton Dene Primary School, Hampton Dene

Pat's Bat

Pat batted a small ball
And it fell to the ground,
Quickly.
Pat fell back onto his hard bat.
Pat broke his leg bone
And shouted loudly, "Argh!"
Nobody came.

Max Thomas (9)
Hampton Dene Primary School, Hampton Dene

Billionaire

A billionaire has so much money,
Lazy like a donkey,
Billionaires are better than millionaires,
Everybody dreams to be a billionaire,
Billionaires can do good and helpful things,
But they also do some working.
They can buy anything,
They can do anything,
It's the coolest.
Billionaires are the happiest,
Wait a minute, this isn't real,
Time to eat my meal.
This is the best dream of my life.
I need a team.
I need to try,
Not to dry.
Why am I sleeping in a bird's nest
Facing west?
Everything is in my imagination and crazy,
It's making me dizzy.
Am I in Dreamland where imagination never ends?

Suba Keerthika Ramachandran (9)
Holy Cross Catholic Primary School, Liverpool

Upside Down

Once upon a dream, I was walking to the sweet shop.
Suddenly, I was upside down.
The hills were upside down like a slide.
The trees were upside down so now I could get the
apples.
The playground was upside down,
I had to sit on my head.
The school was upside down
So now I didn't need to go to school anymore.
I had to walk on my head
And so did everybody else.
The ants looked like black snowmen.
The stars were upside down
And the walls were upside down.
It was difficult to read and write.
My bedroom was upside down,
I had to sleep on the ceiling.
I couldn't put the lights on anymore.

Fatema Abdulbaset Qahtan (9)
Holy Cross Catholic Primary School, Liverpool

The Fallen Kingdom

In the Fallen Kingdom
There is an enchanting rainbow in the bright blue sky.
I can take a nervous, exciting step because of Freedom,
A lake which is frozen dry.

Trees do a handstand
While birds are talking.
This is a crazy dreamland,
Also, flowers are walking.

I figure I am a shape-shifter,
Then I see a backwards castle.
I am a mood lifter,
Also, I win a bizarre raffle.

The Fallen Kindom is as eccentric as a mad scientist,
Actually, I want to be a famous artist.
Suddenly, I am transported to my home in bed
And I hope this dream never fades away.

Aleena Thanawala (10)
Holy Cross Catholic Primary School, Liverpool

Once Upon A Dream

Once upon a dream, many years ago,
Outside it was cold and was covered in white snow.
It was getting late and it was time to go to bed
So let me tell you about the dream that filled my little head.

I was in a fairytale land like no other,
Where everyone was friends and loved each other.
There was no bullying or violence,
This fairytale land just stood in silence.
No one could prepare me for this suspense,
Unicorns, mermaids and rainbows popped out of the sky
And Pegasus and alicorns were soaring so high!
But I soon woke up to realise that it was just a dream!

Miley-May Broadhurst (9)
Holy Cross Catholic Primary School, Liverpool

Nightmares And Dreams!

N ightmares
I n my head,
G oing round and round,
H igh up in the sky, falling
T o my death,
M y head spinning.
A re you a monster?
R olling in my mind,
E verything,
S o blurry

A nd my head aching.
N ow I'm positive,
D reaming away.

D own in a field,
R iding a unicorn,
E verything calm
A nd everything sweet,
M y life,
S o calm.

Lucy-Jo Anders (10)
Holy Spirit Catholic Primary School, Parr

Gymnast Dream

I started a new gymnastics class
With my BFFs, it's going to be a blast.

I walked into the great big hall
With beams and poles, kids small and tall.

I'm excited but I'm nervous, what if I show my belly?
I start to do a cartwheel, I look like a lump of jelly.

Oh no, I think, *I can't do this,*
I'm rubbish and I'm in a tizz.

I see something shining on the floor,
What is it? I wonder, *I need to know.*

I pick it up and it is a ring,
I put it on, it's full of bling.

I start to dance and I am so good,
My legs are straight, like a plank of wood.

I do a handstand, perfectly straight
And do cartwheels six, seven and eight.

The ring is magic, I know it's true,
But then it falls off under someone's shoe.

They shout my name, oh no, it's my turn,
I'll be so bad, I will never learn.

But I take a deep breath and go straight in,
With handstands and dancing, I just need to win.

The ring wasn't magic, it was all in my head,
I was the best dancer, then I woke up in bed!

Bella Leah Ody (9)
Holy Spirit Catholic Primary School, Parr

Greyhound Heaven

Tiptoe down the stairs I come,
There she lies, my delightful beauty
Black as the night, smooth and sleek
Limbs so long they fill her bed.
Strong, powerful, courageous and bright
These are some of my thoughts of her.

Twelve years have passed since we first met
The smile on her face melted my heart
Home she came and filled my life
With hugs, licks and kisses galore
Now I lie beside her bed
Body to body, here we rest.

Then through the field, we leap and bound
Jumping over the swaying grass,
Run, run, run free.

In the distance, I see another, bounding towards us,
delightful and free
Then there we are, all three of us,
On that breathtaking beach, you love.
I look to my left and there I see, another beauty
heading our way

Through the dunes stumbling, I see,
Run, run, run free.

Weaving through the towering trees
Pounding paws crunching leaves,
Faster, faster off they go
Darting here and leaping there,
Panic sweeps as they vanish.
I turn my head and there they stand,
Guarding, another tied to a tree.
Run, run, run free.

I awake with a jolt and face my fear,
There she lies, peaceful and still.
But now I know we've had the best,
Time for you to run, run, run free.

Amélie Roberts (10)
Southdown Primary School, Buckley

What Do I Dream About?

I wonder what I dream about when I rest my head
upon my bed?
"I know," says a voice in my head.
"You dream about flying high in the mythical star
sparkling sky, up, up so high,
With unicorns dancing with their beautiful, flowing hair
And dragons' roars echoing everywhere."
Another voice says, "No, no you don't.
You dream about
Future features and how to make
The world great again, helping the poor and the less
fortunate."
"Oh my! Oh my! You have got it all wrong."
Now I wonder what I dream of.
Each night in the dream, sprites and fairies tell me
different stories.
Do I dream about star-sprinkled sights, dragons and
unicorns,
Up, up so high in the mythical sky?
Or what the world would be like later in life
And helping the poor and the homeless and those with
less?
Maybe I dream about it all a little at a time.
I don't always know what I dream of each night

But I know dreams can come true if you just believe
and sleep tight.
So, just believe in your dreams and all will be right
In your magical dream-filled, star-sprinkled life.

Lilia Molica-Franco (10)

Southdown Primary School, Buckley

Dream On...

I fall asleep lying in my bed,
Bright swirly colours start to fill my head.

A midnight gang, fairies up in a tree
And elephants spraying water at me!

Then a voice pops up inside my head,
"Dream on, young child," it says.

I'm walking on water, flying on land,
Then I'm a snake beneath the sand!

Next, I see a dragon flying up in the sky,
Now I'm a unicorn, oh my, oh my!

Then a voice pops up inside my head,
"Dream on, young child," it says.

I'm hoping and praying this day does not end,
It's so fun leaping and jumping around every bend!

I've made so many friends and had so much fun,
I'll never forget the amazing things I have done!

Then a voice pops up inside my head,
"Dream on, young child," it says.

But then I hear a sound, *ring, ring, ring, ring,*
And wake up to realise I was just dreaming.

Then, wait... what?
It's happening again!

A voice pops up inside my head,
"Dream on, young child," it says.

Mia Broughton
Southdown Primary School, Buckley

Mr Daddy Long Legs

There is a monster under my bed,
What am I going to do?
It has eight long legs and a small body,
What is it doing?

I'm the monster under your bed,
I am your worst nightmare,
Mr Daddy Long Legs is here,
So beware!

I am so scared!
What am I going to do?
Oh no! It's crawling towards me!
What is it doing?

I'm the monster under your bed,
I am your worst nightmare,
Mr Daddy Long Legs is here,
So beware!

I woke up to the sound of my phone buzzing
And I found out it was once upon a dream.

Milly-May Griffiths
Southdown Primary School, Buckley

Incy Wincy Spider!

Me and my pap's love to talk
When we go out on a walk.
We enjoy chattering
Whilst leaves on the floor are crackling.

We came across an eight-legged beast
Looking like we were going to become his midnight
feast...

Mine and my pap's jaws dropped low,
We lowered down like he was wearing a crown.
He started squeaking like mice were weeping,
He said, "Incy wincy spider is growing old
Will you collect me when I turn to gold?"

Lilyann Braithwaite (10)
Southdown Primary School, Buckley

A Flying What?

I stare up to a sky full of midnight stars,
Explosions fill my head in the moonlit sky,
I hear a boom, what can it be?

Crowds cheering for no reason as a... what?
Oh my, oh my, is that a flying pig?
It cannot be!

A grey, flying creature takes over my head,
A hippopotto... what?
It cannot be.

Flying things fill my head
And swirl around like dancing bees.
It's a dream, it just has to be.

A flying what?

Nia Evans
Southdown Primary School, Buckley

Flying High

I wonder how to fly.
How do fairies fly so high?
I tried in the past,
It didn't work on the paths.

Is it your wings that make you fly
Or is it a potion I need to try?
Isn't your power real?
Is it something only you can feel?

As you fly in the sky
The moonlight glistens in your eyes,
As you fly in the sky
The sun shines bright in my eyes.

Tayla Tattersall
Southdown Primary School, Buckley

Dream On

I closed my eyes
And saw the world,
Unicorns, fairies.
I went to pick some berries.

There was a noise,
I opened my eyes to look around.
I heard was a voice saying,
"Dream on, dream on."

I closed my eyes
As tight as can be,
I saw the fairies and
Heard something

The voice said,
"Dream on, dream on."

Evie Cosgrove
Southdown Primary School, Buckley

The Starry Sky!

Bang, I hear a noise,
I'm on a cloud looking around.
Bang, a firework,
Willow!

My little fairy sister,
As cheeky as chickens chuckling like a monkey.
Willow says, "Swing on the vines."
I'm scared.

Whoosh... I grab a vine,
Ha, ha... I love it!
I bounce on clouds
And swing on vines.

I swing onto an orange, sparkling star,
Willow waves her wand.
"Weeeee." The star moves.
Athlete Amy rides the star to the moon,
As cheesy as cheddar cheese.

Swoosh,
I slip off the moon onto a cloud,
Watching the sparkling stars
I fall asleep.
What a dream I had.

Amy Elizabeth Russell (8)
St Andrew's CE (VC) Primary School, Bulmer

Dancing Spider Dream

Bang, bang, bang, came the noise from my window.
Pinch, pinch, pinch, a feeling on my neck.
Turning around, I screamed!
A spider as big as a giant and as scary as a dragon
Tapping me on my neck to get my attention!
A yellow and red sparkly tutu on his back.
I jumped aboard his back when he told me.
Leaping and flying, he took me to a purple ballroom.
Giggle, giggle, giggle, he started doing ballet.
Behind the curtain, *flash*, he was now a wizard as
wonderful as a fairy.
Opening my eyes to a beautiful, bright day.

Emmy Lorraine (8)
St Andrew's CE (VC) Primary School, Bulmer

Driving To The Cheese Moon

Waiting for my car to start,
I am ready for my holiday,
An invisible road in front of me,
I drive forward slowly,
I drive up the magical highway facing towards the
moon.

It looks a long way up
But I still carry on,
I still have at least an hour's journey.

I get my picnic from my seat,
I eat lots of sandwiches,
I rest my feet on the dashboard,
I fall asleep,
My eyes open, glistening at a yellow light,
I'm looking at the cheese moon.

Alfie Caleb Jones (10)
St Andrew's CE (VC) Primary School, Bulmer

Gymnast Nightmare

Opening my eyes, seeing a speck of light.
Spinning around, people on bars, gymnasts all around
me.
Learning to do the splits, I am the best.
Whizz, the grumpy teacher grabs me using magical
powers.
Cobwebs like cotton candy as I land,
A giant spider coming towards me.
Beady eyes looking, sharp pincers clicking!
Fear in my tummy like a bowl of jelly.
Eyes tight shut waiting... waiting.
Peering through slits in my eyes,
It was just a dream.

Orla Beau Sibley (8)
St Andrew's CE (VC) Primary School, Bulmer

Colourful, Magical Woodland

In the magical woodland of fairies, everything is colourful.

Trees are every colour of the rainbow.

Walking on a carpet of red and yellow grass, Kaya and I explore.

We see red squirrels eating nuts at the top of the trees.

Whoosh... Different coloured, sparkly stars float from the trees.

As quick as a flash, fairies appear with dresses matching the trees they left.

Amazingly, a red fairy and a pink fairy came to tell us they are ours.

Rubi Jean Chappell (8)
St Andrew's CE (VC) Primary School, Bulmer

World War II

The sirens as loud as fighting chimpanzees,
Terrified, screeching people sprinted to the tunnel's warmth,
Rooted to the spot like a tree, I was lost
And confused in this madness.

I rapidly sprinted to my shelter,
I was in, I was safe
Or that's what I thought.
Bang! A gas bomb.

The gas was coming, I could hear it.
I had to get out but how?
I had to run...
Or die!

Charlie Banks (10)
St Andrew's CE (VC) Primary School, Bulmer

Stuck In Space

S o much fun,
T rip of a lifetime,
U s floating in space,
C an we keep going?
K eep going, please.

I nstantly floating amongst the stars -
N o one can find us.

S tuck in space forever!
P lease, someone, help us.
A s we see the stars fading away,
C an we find our way back?
E ternally floating...

Tommy Frederick Chappell (10)

St Andrew's CE (VC) Primary School, Bulmer

Facing My Fear

As the wall towers over me like Mount Everest,
I lose my grip,
I fall,
Facing my fear.

My friend gets to the top of the wall rapidly,
He tells me to try again,
I'm on the ground,
I pounce on the wall,
Facing my fear.

I've got confidence,
I get to the top, finally,
I am really proud,
For this day I will never forget,
I faced my fear.

Connor Bickmore (11)
St Andrew's CE (VC) Primary School, Bulmer

Dream Horse

As black as a deep hole,
Her silky, smooth fur glistened in the moonlight.
Her purple eye punctuated her noble face like a full
stop.
Her rough, running feet galloped majestically through
endless space.
Her slowly swaying tail gracefully spun round.
Her long, low, violet mane swayed side to side.
This was a dream horse.

Justin Brown (10)
St Andrew's CE (VC) Primary School, Bulmer

Goal Dreams

My eyes blinking from the hot, yellow sun leaving the
tunnel.
The roar of the crowd filling my ears.
The whistle shouting for us to kick-off!
Excitement giving me energy.

Sprinting like a cheetah, I aimed for goal.
The net caught the ball.
A wave of hands cheering at the goal.
Winning is incredible.

Thomas James Garden (8)
St Andrew's CE (VC) Primary School, Bulmer

The City Logan

As red as a ripe strawberry,
The crimson planet sent chills down my spine.
What lurks behind the emerald-green walls?
Entering the mysterious, green city,
I was praised by clones of me.
What was this unbelievable place?
Each drone telling the story of a year in my life.
Was this strange place once my home?

Logan Pressling (10)
St Andrew's CE (VC) Primary School, Bulmer

Skateboard King

The wind whooshing through my hair
Flying down the quarter pipe.
My heart beating like a drum.
I pop, shove it over the box!

The crowd goes wild,
Adoring fans grappling for my stickers.
A sea of hands waiting for a high-five,
Skating along, slapping hands as I go.

George Griffiths (9)
St Andrew's CE (VC) Primary School, Bulmer

A Perfect World

A perfect world
In my eyes
Would have pure green grass
And bright blue skies.

Pale pink would be the blossoms
That fall off the trees
No small child in the playground
Would ever graze their knees.

The world would be peaceful,
Everyone would be loving,
No hitting, shouting,
Pushing or shoving.

Everyone's feelings
Could be freely expressed
Without being mocked, harassed
Or feeling distressed.

Bunnies would happily hop
Across sunny fields,
Nothing could harm them,
They'd be protected by invisible shields.

Every fantasy inside your head
Would become real,
Every lonely homeless person
Would get a free meal.

The girl slowly put down her pencil,
She sighed,
She went downstairs
And walked outside.

She saw pure green grass,
The sky was bright blue,
Then she realised that her dream had come true.

Faye Elizabeth Joyce Burke (11)
St Joseph The Worker Catholic Primary School, Southdene

Sad Mercury

I go to bed, my eyes go into dream mode,
What is my dream going to be this time?

Why is it cold?
Why is it small here?
Why is there no water?
Why is there no sky?
Why do I feel weightless?
Why do I feel lonely?
Why is there no signal on my phone?

What, what's that glowing light?
I think it's Venus but why's it getting closer?
Are we going to collide?

Mercury,
No,
The planets collide,
I fly over the planet,
I see a boy, "Hello!"

I close my eyes and fall over,
I hear a loud bang,
I wake, and I am actually in bed,
I am relieved that I'm in my room
And in my bed.

Daniel James Gardner (10)
St Patrick's CE Primary School, Endmoor

Little Dreamer

Clowns, clown around in the dead of night,
Gave me a shiver down my spine and a terrible fright.
One gave me a red balloon,
Spookily, it was a full moon,
Now it's 3am,
Wish I was home in bed.

He took me somewhere new.
I wish this land was true.
What I saw before my eyes,
Little fairies and white butterflies.
I saw Easter eggs and candyfloss trees,
Next, I saw a big slide, made me go, weeee.

He took me back to my small bedroom,
Gave me a hug and my cat a groom.

"Goodnight little dreamer," said the clown,
"Never again visit my lost town."

Holly Ellis (9)
St Patrick's CE Primary School, Endmoor

My Dream

I once had a dream about myself,
I dreamt about my teddy bear sat upon a shelf.
I was cosy in my bed like a cuddly sloth.
My house was the size of the Milky Way,
With sticky toffee chairs which grew back when you ate them.
Its walls were made of sweet-smelling logs.
The magical garden was as big as a football pitch
And was made of sticky, green sweets.
Then the tap slowly went *drip, slurp, whoosh, pop, pow,*
The tap broke, *bang, crash!*
As through the window, the moon winked at me.
I didn't want to wake but I had to, it was morning.

Poppy Easterlow (10)
St Patrick's CE Primary School, Endmoor

Transported

Suddenly, I'm here,
In this strange new place,
I look above the horizon
And see many things.

First, there is a mountain,
High up in the sky,
But also great big canyons,
Sinking down below.

Suddenly, I realise
Where this strange place is.
It is the red planet,
Rusty and alone.

After I hear a monstrous noise,
An asteroid whirling past,
Next a huge supernova
Exploding close by.

Then I am knocked off my feet,
Towards Valles Marineris.
Falling, falling, falling,
4.3 miles deep.

Erin Munford (9)
St Patrick's CE Primary School, Endmoor

Dreaming

D reaming away, The Island Of Illusion is on its way

R acing towards him, he knows that he will turn into a newt

E erie noises are close and he may clothe himself with fear

A bright light chases the island away, I must give chase

M esmerised at a nebular being born like a letter being torn

I must think about how to get out

N ever before have I seen such trouble I have been in

G etting up, I go and play with my pup.

Ben Morris (9)
St Patrick's CE Primary School, Endmoor

Dancing

D ancing in the studio with my friends

A s I feel eyes watching me dance.

N ow we all sense that something is going to happen.

C lowns come rushing out of the mirror,

I 'm filled with fear!

"N o!" I scream as the clowns push us into the mirror,

G rabbing my arm as they try to stop me from breathing, luckily it was all a dream.

Abby Mason (10)

St Patrick's CE Primary School, Endmoor

Perdie Pony

P erdie is the best pony in the whole wide world
E very day, Perdie Pony has to deal with
R iding
D an is Perdie's friend
I love her so much
E very day I see her, I am so happy

P erdie is healthy and safe
O wen is Perdie's friend too
N ever will I sell her
Y ou might ride her.

Samantha Taylor (8)
St Patrick's CE Primary School, Endmoor

Dream

D reams are special
R oller skating at home
E xcited to go on holiday
A m going on a plane
M y mum gave me mashed potatoes.

Kieran Collier (9)
St Patrick's CE Primary School, Endmoor

Claustrophobia

C laustrophobia, a thing we all hate,

L ately, its been disturbing me; I can't go on at this rate.

A ll our mouths panic, mine panics to a phobia,

U sually, I'm fine, but my head's going to dystopia.

S ometimes it's rotten, sometimes it's crazy,

T he thought of claustrophobia makes me a little dazy.

R oses are red, violets are blue,

O ver my brain comes the phobia flu.

P eople are different in many ways,

H aving this curse has been killing me for days.

O thers may not know what I do,

B arriers block my escape and I have no clue.

I feel it eating me up inside,

A nother day with claustrophobia, but I still have to hide...

Chloc Tuan Darcy-Langley (10)

Tattingstone Primary School, Tattingstone

My Dream

I am on the back of my dragon,
Soaring through the wind,
On our way to Tanazia,
Our wonderful home,
My hair flowing,
As my dragon's wings beat against my legs,
I do this every day,
In the hope of finding something new,
New dragons are our goal,
We have to fly carefully,
We aren't alone,
For in these waters
A foe is always ready,
Dragon hunters,
They have a fleet of ships,
Arrows tipped with dragon root,
A substance that could overwhelm a dragon
completely,
Nets that no dragon could escape,
If they get caught
Who knows what will happen?
That is why we are here,
To stop these people
Once and for all.

Olive Potter-Cobbold (11)
Tattingstone Primary School, Tattingstone

Harry Potter

H arry Potter is as magical as a unicorn,

A s I step to the train, *fizz, swish, whizz,* go wands,

R eally excited as I get my first glimpse,

R ely on Hogwarts to make my dream come true,

Y et I wade my way through wands flying through the air.

"P ut on your robes, we'll be there soon."

O ther students, big and small, arriving now,

T hat is a spectacular sight.

T he Sorting Hat is ready for me,

E ating in the Great Hall,

R eally, I don't want to wake but morning comes and it's over. I'll never dream again.

Faith Davy (9)
Tattingstone Primary School, Tattingstone

Swimming Pools

S un is making the pool burning hot.

W aves are calm.

I ce is melting and making the water stone-cold.

M um is jumping like crazy.

M oon is reflecting the pool, wow!

I nflatables are being jumped on, ow!

N ow we're here, we swish to the pool, weee!

G ames are sinking to the bottom of the black ditch pool.

P eople are excited to go to the pool.

O ceans are flying like mad.

O pen water is freezing.

L ilies are in the pool.

S wimming pools are the best, ahhh, so relaxing!

Jack Harry Hemsley Cooper (8)

Tattingstone Primary School, Tattingstone

My Wacky Dream

First, I see my teddy bear, dancing on the floor,
Then I hear a knock and there's an orange at the door,
He comes inside and knocks over my decaf tea,
Next, the puddle on the floor turns into the sea.

I see multicoloured waves that are lapping next to us,
Suddenly, there is a sound and out of nowhere comes a bus,
We jump on board and I sit in my seat,
I notice that the driver is a giant and has very smelly feet,
"Woah!" I say as we dive into a tunnel that is very red,
Immediately, with shock, I wake up in my cosy bed.

Francesca Goodwin (11)
Tattingstone Primary School, Tattingstone

The Famous Superhero

On a new stage,
In a new town,
I arrived,
I performed on the brand-new stage,
And became famous.

Then, a day later, I ran
On the top of buildings
And fell into a room,
Full of wonder and fun.
Then some sticky slime stuff came
And fell on top of me
And I turned into a superhero
With lots of powers.

Samuel Cocksedge (10)
Tattingstone Primary School, Tattingstone

Mauritius

M eringues to eat,

A pples to chew and grow; *squelch,*

U mbrellas to throw out,

R ain is warm; *splash,*

I nteresting fruit to try,

T hunder to hear; *fuzz, bang!*

I nteresting bugs to hear,

U nder the leaves lie bugs,

S ea is as warm as a bath.

Daisy Kemp (9)
Tattingstone Primary School, Tattingstone

Anxiety

A nxiety, fear,

N ever-ending depression,

X anax tablets at the ready, every ten minutes,

I ndividual feeling with no one to help,

E verywhere I go is a never-ending pit of darkness,

T ime goes by as I slowly wilt away to nothing,

Y ears go by as I slowly but sadly stay the same.

James Moore (10)
Tattingstone Primary School, Tattingstone

Once Upon A Dream

Once upon a dream ago,
I loved dancing and prancing,
In a show
I saw a girl called Britney,
She taught me how to turn
As fast as a cheetah can learn.
Once upon a dream ago
I was as famous as a TV show.
Whoosh!

Aggie Cook (9)
Tattingstone Primary School, Tattingstone

Spring

(A kennings poem)

Hedgehogs-hiding
Leaves-falling
Winter-ending
Life-starting
Birds-singing
Sand-warming
Fetes-starting
Fun-beginning.

Charles Peter Hemsley Cooper (10)
Tattingstone Primary School, Tattingstone

The Dream

In this grey, misty room
Full of gloom,
Search for any signs of life,
But this is all pain and strife.

Thud! What was that?
Is this a joke?
I hope this is because...
I just felt a poke!

Stumbling through the hall of clowns,
With no clue what's around,
This is the hall of terrors
Or the shop of horrors.

I fall into the hall of death
Just coming to the end,
Then I tumble down a hole
And then I'm back in bed!

Poppy Louise Marion Kirkwood (10)
Templeton CP School, Templeton

Horror Wonderland

I went to Winter Wonderland
With a guy called Steve.
He had never been scared before.
When we got there, it was as dark as coal!
Steve went in, then ran away in tears!
I went in...
At first, I thought it was a trick...
But the logo said, 'Horror Wonderland'.
Then my legs were as wobbly as a wobbly chair!
Then a clown said, "Hi!"
After, I thought, *this is not so scary.*
But then...
The clown was holding a very sharp knife!
I got so scared that I woke up.
I said in my head, *that was a bad dream.*

Harry Howell (9)
Tonysguboriau Primary School, Talbot Green

Recycle, Recycle

As I sleep silently below the clouds like a baby,
I dribble while my thoughts dramatically crumble.
A flicker of a giant monster gobbling up the city
I now live in.

Five years later, there has been a break out in England,
I looked out of the window,
I see a massive bin monster cleaning the world?

OMG, now it's eating people with a sign of 'People
Recycle' on the belly of the beast

The beast is growing

There have been clips of the creature moaning and
screeching in pain when it eats plastic

We load the whole thing into a chamber with tons of
plastic
On activation, it releases a pungent toxic scent
Slipping through the breathing holes
Suffocating us all

But the beast was fading

And the plastic and the filth is still haunting us to this
very day.

Elias Wright (10)
Trowell CE Primary School, Trowell

In The Land Of Fantasy

While children sleep, the dreams sneak across the
flying sky,
But then, thumping little elephants let out a little cry,
As the planets wade the ocean, ever-so-deep across
the space-lit sky,
Your grandma comes hobbling over to say a happy
goodbye.

The nightmares shall weep while the dreams leak,
Under the delicate silk of your mind,
But you have to remember this world isn't round,
It's frankly very crowned.

Though the sun may be an orange,
The music shall dance through the midnight gust.
The beams of light sprayed from a firefly exploded to
and fro,
The moon lit up with a flicker of a dove floating fairly
high,
The thunder shall flick with the flick of a switch from a
firefly.

But something was wrong, the clouds were grey,
The birds at bay now, what a horrible day,
The horses aren't going neigh
While people pray.

Until someone said, "We need to climb the glistening, moonlit sky,
To find what is nigh in the sky."
We made it to where dreams scream
And nightmares jump around in glee
To where unicorns are set on fire
And the clock will ring every hour.

With the blood-red sky flying high,
All the nightmares were sent to die,
One by one, happy or gone,
They disappeared from this magical wrong.

Like all fairy tales, it ends with thy
To let the dream fly high.

Aidan Smart (10)
Trowell CE Primary School, Trowell

Sandman's Journey

It's Sandman's duty
To take you to the strange Land of Beauty,
That you call a dream.
He drifts through the place where the stars always gleam,
Then he arrives at the ivory gate.
The dreamland and human world, it does separate,
The workers see him in his golden grace
And open the gate so there is a space.

He nods his thanks to the gatekeepers,
Then he's off on his mission to help the human sleepers.
Babies are tucked up in their cosy cots,
Children in bunk beds and singles,
Sandman's whole body tingles,
His magic awakens and is suddenly alive.
He knows what to do... It's time for the dreams to thrive!
A beautiful, prancing unicorn
With a shimmering, golden horn
And seeing the children smile
Makes Sandman's tricky job worth the while.

After a night of hard work,
He floated back through the dark night's murk,
Back through the now sunlit gate,
It's morning and a new date -
It's night for Sandman, time for his rest.

Now, when you have a dream,
Remember who gave it to you,
What Sandman did, what he can do.

Poppy Gow (10)

Trowell CE Primary School, Trowell

Things That Used To Be

When I lay my head on my pillow, I see my old street,
The trees, the canal, the birds that tweet.
The sky is like the deep blue sea,
The clouds always wave and give me company.

My bedroom is small but cute, only room for one, not two,
My next-door neighbours scream and shout,
"Come out, come out! Rosie, come out!"
We'd play all day and just for a treat
My magnificent mum would get us sweets.

When I went to my grandad's castle-like house,
My grandma would be there, as quiet as a mouse,
It's even quieter now because she's not there,
But I can still feel her loving care.

Sophie was a dog with one eye, not two,
When you'd stroke her she'd jump right up at you,
She has passed because her frail body didn't last,
But her bark is a song stuck in your head.
My pillow is her soft dog bed.

Things that used to be will always be a helping hand and help me,

Now I've woken up and can't remember a thing,
It's funny how we can't remember our dreams.

Rosanna Race (10)

Trowell CE Primary School, Trowell

Whizz! Bang! Bang!

As my head hit the pillow,
I saw my gingerbread house.
You would eat it if you had very little.
On the left, I saw the chocolate lake,
It was so yummy to drink.

Then I saw the Wicked Witch of the West,
"Whizz, bang, bang!" she cried.
I was scared,
My heart was a furious lion.

Everywhere I looked I saw her name all over,
Killer clowns now roamed the streets,
Wearing their crimson-red noses,
Death walked down the alleyway.

I ran down the cold avenue,
Holding what used to be a lollipop stick.
Suddenly, they were there,
The killer clowns.

They were running after me like a tornado,
Scared, solemn and sour, I threw my lollipop stick at
them.
"Help!" I yelled.
Then *snap!* My eyes shot open.

I was safe at home!
My doll's house was still there. "Phew!"
My doll was still there. "Phew!"
My dreamcatcher was still there. "Phew!"
But where did the eyes come from?

Ava Byrne (9)
Trowell CE Primary School, Trowell

In The Land Of Nod...

The stars are tiny marbles scattered on a child's floor,
The sunset is a flickering light bulb that isn't used
anymore.
The violent wind is like a fan on full speed,
It would be hard for me to hold a dog's lead.

Daft dragons dig deep
And find curious cats trying to be clever and creep.
Happiness dives here and there,
I am so glad it is not a terrible nightmare.

I see the sun sneaking
Among clever clouds
Like a wild, terrific tiger.

All of a sudden, it turns dark and scary
And all the stars turn dull and weary.
The sunset is the same,
None of this is now a game.

I stare at the windswept wind weeping
Above the poor people
Like a constant rain.

I close my eyes
To say bye-bye,

Then I see my bedroom floor
Above my bedroom door.

Millie Concannon (10)
Trowell CE Primary School, Trowell

What Wonderful Things You Can Find In A Galaxy

As the sun sets and no longer smiles,
The stars rise
And the galaxy swims as deep as the sea.

Rebel rabbits refuse to run rapidly,
Famous fish fashionably flipping frantically,
The happy hippos and bouncing bunnies,
Oh, what wonderful things you can find in a galaxy.

When I look up, I wonder,
Have I been here before?
Why can't I feel my body?
Why are the stars singing?
Is this even real?

Stars sing like a soothing whistle,
Daytime dances like an elegant eagle,
Butterflies bounce like a beautiful bunny,
Oh, what wonderful things you can find in a galaxy.

Now you've been in the Land of Nod,
Hopefully, you will visit there too,
Maybe you will dream of unicorns
Or even dancing dinosaurs.

Hannah Martin (10)
Trowell CE Primary School, Trowell

My Dog Is A Dog

When I finally started dreaming
That I got a real dog of my own,
Of course, I was glad
That I was no longer alone,
But also, in the end, it had
Been good to be without a friend,
As it made me see
How wonderful life could be.
My dream dog dances adorably
Like a pro-rugby player - *bang, crash, scatter!*
My dream dog likes pretty much everything
Like my perfect pies and pigeons for dessert.
My dream dog loves to watch 'Ratatouille'!
Because he thinks the rat is a cat!
Sadly, it was all a dream,
But it was pretty sweet.
Now I finally have no dog barking at the window,
Now it is with my grandma and grandad
Swishing and swaying in the wind
Even though I still feel their spirits right over.

Theo James Morgan (10)
Trowell CE Primary School, Trowell

A World Of Weirdness!

I dream of words whizzing;
They're like speedy jets,
It's as if I'm in a world of weirdness.

I take a look around;
I see words forming my name,
It spells L-e-i-l-a.

In this world of colour;
Each word is different,
This is the story of my name.

L stands for lovely yellow,
I see lemons;
Luscious, lively lemons.

E stands for emerald,
I see a lake;
Deep, dark, dangerous emerald.

I stands for indigo,
I see a bunch of grapes;
Glamorous globes ready to be gobbled up.

L stands for lime-green,
I see lollipops;
Lovely, lickable lollipops.

Am I swirling or are the words?
I freeze!
My alarm goes off.

Leila Burt (10)
Trowell CE Primary School, Trowell

In The Calm Midnight World

In the calm, midnight world
There is a midnight sky with little stars winking
And giving you company.

All the children sleep like pearls
And dream about them going in a dream world
Like they are entering a land of beauty.

They all wake up in an enchanted forest
And hear a soft, sweet voice saying,
"Come out of your cosy cottage!"

In the magical, angelic forest there is golden dust
Filled with magic and chubby, fluffy bears
With a basket full of sparkly magic dust.

As quickly as it had begun
The world was collapsing one by one.
"Please don't go!" said the baby brown bears
But the dream world was gone and there was silence.

Ben Small (10)
Trowell CE Primary School, Trowell

The Future!

When I go to sleep at night,
All the fears that were before,
Don't exist anymore.
Then I sense an open door,
This makes me want to scream,
Then I remember it's only a dream.

I walked through without a care
To find a spaceship, old and bare.
I went aboard, wanting a sword for the journey ahead,
I went up and away, above and beyond,
Hoping I would live another day.

I saw the Great Wall of China finally collapse,
I felt in the distance there were booby traps.
Big Ben chimed once more.
Paris shut down and there was a hole to the Earth's core!
Bad things are coming!
Children everywhere, the apocalypse is real, so best beware!

Tia-Madison Ingham (10)
Trowell CE Primary School, Trowell

Penguins On Ice

Every penguin's mum
Can toboggan on her tum.
She can only do that
As she's fluffy and fat.

It must be nice
To live on ice.

Every penguin's dad
Is happy and glad.
He can slip and slide
And swim and glide.

It must be nice
To live on ice.

All penguin chicks
Do slippery tricks.
They sway and fall
But don't mind at all.

It must be nice
To live on ice.

I dream of a world like an iceberg,
The land like a sun made of ice.
Penguins plopping peacefully

In and out of the sea.

It must be nice
To live on ice.

How lucky are those penguins on ice?

Logan Jones (10)
Trowell CE Primary School, Trowell

Nightmare

In the World of Dreams,
Things aren't always bright and cheerful!
Sometimes darkness rules
And there are demons and ghouls.

Sometimes the pain is the sharp teeth,
Pierced in your skin
And the evil is your sin.

Sometimes the World of Dreams
Is as black as venom,
Sometimes this darkness
Is a devious devil gobbling you up.

Sometimes broken buildings tower above,
All strong and tough.
Maybe the wind is a howling wolf, scary and rough.

Sometimes there is a ghost,
Perhaps hanging out on the east coast?

The shadow could be your dark reflection,
Darker than a zombie resurrection.

Charlie Partridge (10)
Trowell CE Primary School, Trowell

Dreams

As I snuggled into bed that night,
A million things filled my eyes,
I travelled to the Land of Nod,
Where dreams are real.

I've been here before with my friend, Unicorn,
Who helps me in my dreams,
His silver horn shimmers and shines
Just like a spectacular star.

Rainbow colours blind my eyes,
Spots and patches too,
They twist, turn and swirl through the night
Just like a tornado.

We hop on clouds,
Run over rainbows,
Dance beneath the sun.

As I place my head on the unicorn's mane
A million things fill my eyes,
I travel back from the Land of Nod
Where dreams are real.

Rosie Turnbull (10)
Trowell CE Primary School, Trowell

Magical Mystery

In my mysterious dream
I see a gorgeous, glistening waterfall
Singing loudly
Like a glamorous model.

Inside the stunning waterfall
Is a little, wooden cabin screaming dramatically
Like an old lady.

Within the aged cabin
Is a wide, grey cauldron, that whispers calmly
Like a hungry beggar.

Through the broad cauldron
Is nothing but a wizard,
Who tells me quietly
To keep this magical mystery a secret.

Suddenly, I woke up.

Clarice Edmonds (10)
Trowell CE Primary School, Trowell

Spoons Of Candy Land

I dream of silver spoons soaring
Above the crazy Candy Land
Like a million fireflies.

Spontaneous spoons take place in the SK Candy Land marathon,
Through Candy Cane Cave
Like a crowd of people.

Sassy spoons
Walk slowly and munch on the scrumptious candy
Like a hungry herd of elephants.

The shiny spoons start to talk
Underneath the red, liquorice ground to a candy tree -
Which is made out of marshmallows
Like an imaginary friend.

Bella Marie Turner (10)
Trowell CE Primary School, Trowell

Temmingtoo, The City Of Dreams

I dream of opening the full moon door,
Beneath me was the City of Dreams
Like the door of peace.

I dream of a land swimming through the galaxy,
In the City of Dreams, Temmingtoo,
Like fireflies buzzing wildly.

I dream of upside down animals running rapidly
Beneath the light blue sky
Like a black vampire bat.

I dream of a spiral staircase twisting and turning
Above the City of Dreams,
Like a beautiful, enchanted galaxy.

Poppy Potts-Padgett (9)
Trowell CE Primary School, Trowell

In The Land Of Nod

In the Land of Nod
There are tall trees soaring over a few feet.
The little land is a flower garland,
The gritty grass is now shining like brass
Near clouds of blue and crowned,
Wondrous wind whistling willingly.

Big buildings bishing and bashing,
Thrashing and mashing.
The sky is a soft sheet of silk giving tasty milk.
Terrific towers turning thoughtfully,
Oh no, it's getting bright,
I hope you have a good night.

Mohammad Ali Saddique (10)
Trowell CE Primary School, Trowell

Dancing Dinosaur Dreams

I dream of a dancing dinosaur
Leaping over naughty New York
Like an astronaut.

I dream of a famous dragon
Bouncing up to a super slide
Like a pirate.

I dream of flying fish
Disappearing towards a magnificent moon
Like a zooming rocket.

I dream of a trustworthy tiger
Traipsing through trees
Like a bull.

Freya Noakes (9)
Trowell CE Primary School, Trowell

Centre Of The Earth Theme Park

T oday, I went to a theme park

"H elp me, I am too small to go on most rides but my brother is way bigger."

E ducation is needed to come here.

T o get here, you need to use a digger

"H elp me understand," you may ask. The theme park is underground.

E ven though it was expensive, it was worth the money.

M y favourite ride is 'The Terror',

E ven though I would never go on it again, never!

P erfect this ride is, the perfect size for me,

A ltogether we said, "Cheese!" The perfect family photo.

R ockets, we went home in rockets.

K *aboom*, we were off. Happily heading to bed.

Ruby Grace Cowan (8)
Victoria Junior School, Workington

My Teacher Is A Spy!

I was walking to school and I heard the bell,
It was so loud it frightened me, so I fell.
When I looked up in the sky
I noticed something, it looked like a spy.
I looked again and she could fly,
When I went to school, I looked at my teacher,
She looked exactly like the spy
Who was in the sky.

I followed my teacher home,
She came to a big glass office, I looked up
And I was in luck, it was the Spy Office,
I knew my teacher was a spy,
The one that could fly in the sky.
I saw spies everywhere,
They could fly in the sky very high.
I found a jetpack, I put it on,
I went out and I tried to fly like a spy
But I got stuck and fell in some muck, yuck!

Aimee Marie Benson (7)
Victoria Junior School, Workington

The Magical Unicorn

My unicorn is called Katy,
She's not just any unicorn
She's a magical unicorn,
Let me tell you why?

She gave me magic powers
So I could fly with her too.
We flew all around the world
And went on lots of holidays.

Katy is so, so cool,
We flew together all night,
We flew to lots of different countries,
I had such a good time.

But in the morning I realised
It was all just a dream,
Although it felt so real,
I miss Katy.

Summer Carr (7)
Victoria Junior School, Workington

Harry Potter

Harry Potter is awesome,
Just like you,
I've watched all the movies
And you should too.

Harry Potter is the best
And you should know,
'Deathly Hallows' is my favourite,
You would watch the show.

In my dreams
There was Harry Potter,
He came into my room
And made a big clutter.

He started doing spells,
He waved his wand.
"Lumos Holem," he cried
And my room turned into a pond.

Alisha Hussain (8)
Victoria Junior School, Workington

Liverpool Fun

I was playing football with Liverpool
Against Man United and we won,
Then some alien ships came
And it started to get fun.

Then water monsters joined us
With their blue, fuzzy hair,
Next, I looked ahead of me
And I was frightened by a bear.

I found a laser sniper
So I lasered them all away,
I can't wait to play again for Liverpool,
Hopefully on a normal day.

Blake Dakin (8)
Victoria Junior School, Workington

Unicorn Fun

U nicorns are smart and bright.

N ever so bright and happy at night.

I gnore all the nightmares and have some fun.

C ome and play out with us in the sun!

O range juice helps when you're sweaty.

R un on the clouds like crazy.

N ever do nothing,

S o come up to us and let's do some dancing!

Julia Kuder (8)

Victoria Junior School, Workington

I Am A Liverpool Player

JOnce upon a dream
I played football for Liverpool at Anfield.
When I got there, I forgot my kit
So I had to go home.

When I got home, it wasn't there,
I looked everywhere for it.
Suddenly, I looked out of my window,
There was my dog, Diesel, in my kit.

C J Moore
Victoria Junior School, Workington

A Unicorn Appears

The unicorn's horn is made out of corn.
The colours are pink, purple and blue.
The mane is multicoloured with a nice bright hue.
It has fluffy, puffy fur.
I climb up on this magical beast
And then we take flight up in the sky.
Then we fly, fly, fly in the sky.

Alaiya Richardson (8)
Victoria Junior School, Workington

The Magic Wizard

My dream is about a wizard,
He grants me wishes.
I asked for a pet hamster,
But instead, he sent me fishes.

"Oh, wizard," I cried,
"This is the wrong wish!"
"I'm sorry!" he said
And my hamster appeared in a dish.

Lacey-Leigh Harding (7)
Victoria Junior School, Workington

I Saw A Cool Motorbike

In my dream, I saw a red motorbike.
I was so shocked I nearly passed out!
I rode the motorbike all night,
It was so, so cool.

I was so happy,
I wish it was real-life,
But I realised it wasn't
When I woke up in my bed.

Archie Smitham (7)
Victoria Junior School, Workington

The People

The people have powers.
The people can fly.
They can fly really fast.
They run everywhere.
The cars can fly
And the bus.
Everything can fly in my dream.

Song Song Chen (8)
Victoria Junior School, Workington

Spiders In My Dream

Once upon a dream
I saw some spiders.
They gave me a fright,
Turns out they were nice.

Kyron Knowles (8)
Victoria Junior School, Workington

Unicorn And Me

I was walking through the clouds until I came to a stop.
All of a sudden, I saw a unicorn and my heart went
pop!
Unicorns are so pretty, glittery and fair
With their horns so golden and beautiful long hair.
The unicorn looked at me and said with a smile,
"Will you be my friend and stay with me a while?"
The unicorn and I played all day long,
Skipping through the sky and singing a song.
The unicorn and I stayed up all night,
Telling each other stories until the sun came up bright.
When it was time for me to go,
For me to see the unicorn again, I just have to look out
of my window.

Lily Bavister (8)
West Grantham Academy St John's, Grantham

Unicorn Land

Hey Miss Unicorn,
You look very nice.
I like your gold horn,
Can you eat rice?

I like your candy house,
I can hear your bell.
The clouds look like candyfloss,
I think I know you very well.

I want some unicorn friends.
Can you read my mind?
I have human friends but not unicorn ones,
Your wings shine.

Roksana Osowska (8)
West Grantham Academy St John's, Grantham

Imaginary Creatures

I maginary creatures
M ulticoloured unicorns prancing in the grass
A night dragon's wings
G oing *whoosh, beat, whoosh, beat*
I magination running free
N o limit to it
A licorns flock together
R eady to migrate for better weather
Y ou will see them in your dreams.

C reatures are amazing
R eady for a fight
E verlasting beauty
A nd heading for the night
T urn around in your dreams
U ntil you see...
R ulers of the day and night
E verlasting power
S ecretive and strong.

Annabel Syme (8)
Wyndham Primary Academy, Alvaston

Mythical Creatures

M ythical creatures
Y ummy unicorn sweets
T he unicorns have
H appy unicorn
I magination
C lever unicorns
A ll unicorns are friends
L oving unicorns.

C lean, fluffy unicorns
R ainbows are everywhere
E xtraordinary
A ll unicorns are cute
T ogether, unicorns play
U seful unicorn
R eally beautiful unicorns
E xcellent unicorns
S prinkles come out of unicorns' bottoms.

Sophia Sylvia (7)
Wyndham Primary Academy, Alvaston

Games, Games, Games!

Games, games, games,
Why do you always glitch?
I would rather eat Romanian mitch.

Games, games, games,
Why do you always glitch?
I could watch YouTube
And look, I have a new tooth!

Games, games, games,
Why do you always glitch?
I will throw you away!

Alvin Nkwelle (8)
Wyndham Primary Academy, Alvaston

Dreams

D reams fill my head and I love them too much
R are as red and gold diamonds
E very night, I fall asleep and carry on with my dream
A lways dreaming for quite a while
M inecraft is my favourite dream
S o amazing, they might come true.

Toby Elijah Walsh (7)
Wyndham Primary Academy, Alvaston

Dreams

D reams of money as bright as gold
R are rubies as red as cherries
E at runny honey that you love
A maze the crowd that you know
M y dreams will come true if I pray
S omething will come into my head if I try.

Gabrielle Orunmuyi (8)

Wyndham Primary Academy, Alvaston

Dreams

D reams fill my mind, night and day

R espect your dreams at night-time

E very day, I can't wait for the night so I see my dream

A lways want to see or do more dreams

M y dreams are going to be good and beautiful.

Julia Cybulska (8)
Wyndham Primary Academy, Alvaston

Nature

N ever-ending, just like a sphere

A stonishing as a hooked-nosed sea snake

T errific when day turns to night

U nderstanding animals around

R eal-life and not just

E xciting when day turns to night.

Beth Rule (8)

Wyndham Primary Academy, Alvaston

Dreams

D reams fill my mind with horses and diamonds
R ubies fill the grass and sun
E very night, I cannot wait to dream
A lways waiting when it's dark
M y eyes will close and the dream will start.

Laura Viktorija Klaveniece (7)
Wyndham Primary Academy, Alvaston

Dreams

D ream about the people you love and care for

R oses are red

E very night, I can't wait to dream

A lways dream about a different thing

M y dreams can always be with love.

Kelsey Biddle (8)

Wyndham Primary Academy, Alvaston

Dreams

D reams of being a unicorn
R oses are red, violets are blue. How will I pick you?
E very night, I cannot wait to dream
A lways wanting more
M y dreams will come true.

Lily-May Wosik (8)
Wyndham Primary Academy, Alvaston

Dreams

D reams of money as rich as gold
R are rubies as red as roses
E very night, I'm so pumped to dream
A lways wanting more from my mind
M y dreams will never die.

Lily Harrison (8)
Wyndham Primary Academy, Alvaston

Dreams

D reaming of unicorns
R oses are red, violets are blue, who will pick you?
E very night, I can't wait for tomorrow
A lways be nice
M y dream is true.

Emily Neimane (8)
Wyndham Primary Academy, Alvaston

Mutants

M arvellous mascots
U niversal threats
T remendous fighters
A nd very silly
N otorious villains
T ricky tricksters
S illy Billies.

Michael Turner (8)
Wyndham Primary Academy, Alvaston

Dreams

D ream of lots, use your imagination
R ed rubies fill my mind at night
E very night, I cannot wait to dream
A lways want more
M y dream will come true.

Dylan Adkins (8)
Wyndham Primary Academy, Alvaston

Dreams

D ream about being an amazing dodgeball player
R are like red rubies
E very night, I love to dream
A lways love dreaming
M y dreams may come to life.

Harry Woolley (8)
Wyndham Primary Academy, Alvaston

Holidays

H appy sounds
O n the beach
L istening to the sound
I ce creams melt
D ancing waves
A ll around us
Y ellow sand on the ground.

John Holmes (8)
Wyndham Primary Academy, Alvaston

Dream

D reams fill my mind at night-time
R are like a red ruby
E very night, I can't wait to dream
A lways wanting more
M y dreams will come true.

Cole Ingman (8)

Wyndham Primary Academy, Alvaston

Dreams

D reams fill my mind at night-time
R are like red rubies
E very night, I cannot wait to dream
A lways wanting more
M y dreams will come true.

Rakeisha Vuyelwa Mutandi (8), Edgar & Nenidawh
Wyndham Primary Academy, Alvaston

Dreams

D reams fill my mind at night-time
R are like a red stone
E very day, I have a dream
A lways want more
M y dream will come true.

Jonatan Domzala (8)
Wyndham Primary Academy, Alvaston

Games

G listening, pretty homes
A nnoyed people shouting
M arlie and his friends
E njoying their fun
S plashing in the water.

Marlie James Doniel Shields (8)
Wyndham Primary Academy, Alvaston

Dreams

D reams matter in my head
R are like red rubies
E very night, I dream
A lways in for more
M y dreams are nice.

Alfie Welch (7)
Wyndham Primary Academy, Alvaston

Happy

H ugging blanket
A s happy as a ladybug
P laying in the sun
P erfect plants
Y ummy candy and chocolate.

Isabelle Saxby (8)
Wyndham Primary Academy, Alvaston

Dogs

D ogs barking
O lly's best friends
G ood girls
S it down, dogs.

Olly Benjamin (8)

Wyndham Primary Academy, Alvaston

Dogs

D ogs are okay

O n a mat

G o to bed

S o many dogs.

Keegan Morris (8)
Wyndham Primary Academy, Alvaston

The Clown

Drifting away on a cloud,
To where the phantoms and ghouls are found,
No pictures are so bold and bright,
Frightening thoughts through the night.

His yellow teeth and blood-red smile
Grinning at me for a while.
Big black eyes and his face all white
Enough to give my heart a fright.

The clown, he watches me for a while,
Nothing funny in that smile.
I turn to run far away,
This clown, he doesn't want to play.

I cannot breathe, the clown is coming,
I hear a scream, my heart is drumming.
I twist and turn in my bed,
The scream was only in my head.

Arrin Riccards (9)
Ysgol Parcyrhun, Ammanford

The Dream

T he thing about my dream is that it's funny
H orses and cows who love honey
E lecorns and winged monkeys, I'm not sure are a thing

D ancing rainbows and fireplaces with some bling
R aining candy out from the sky
E verlasting gobstoppers the size of a pie
A lot of people in my dream play rugby on boring old grass
M e, when I don't play rugby on grass, I play with sass.

Olivia Tozer (11)
Ysgol Parcyrhun, Ammanford

Unicorns

U nusual creatures, these things are

N o one knows really how far

I n the kingdoms, they will always stay

C astles upon hills, that's where they play

O f course, unicorns are colourful and bright

R iding under the silhouette of moonlight

N ow night has finally come

S leep well, my unicorn, until the sun.

Harriet Tozer (8)

Ysgol Parcyrhun, Ammanford

Pirate

P irate ships will sail the seas
I wish I was a pirate with all that fortune
R eminiscing about past adventures
A ny adventure we may have done, even if it wasn't all fun
T reasure found by following a map
E very day, we will hunt for our fortune.

Olivia Anne Griffiths (8)
Ysgol Parcyrhun, Ammanford

Est.1991

YOUNG WRITERS
INFORMATION

We hope you have enjoyed reading this book – and
that you will continue to in the coming years.

If you're a young writer who enjoys reading and creative writing,
or the parent of an enthusiastic poet or story writer,
do visit our website **www.youngwriters.co.uk**. Here you will
find free competitions, workshops and games, as well as
recommended reads, a poetry glossary and our blog.

If you would like to order further copies of this book,
or any of our other titles, then please give us a
call or visit **www.youngwriters.co.uk**.

Young Writers
Remus House
Coltsfoot Drive
Peterborough
PE2 9BF
(01733) 890066
info@youngwriters.co.uk